EASTER FUN

Activity B

by Judith Stampe.

Illustrated by Julie Durrell

METRIC EQUIVALENTS

1 inch = 2.54 centimeters
1 square inch = 6.45 square centimeters
1 foot = 30.5 centimeters

1 teaspoon = 5 milliliters (approx.)
1 tablespoon = 15 milliliters (approx.)
1 fluid ounce = 29.6 milliliters
1 cup = .24 liter
1 pint = .47 liter
1 quart = .95 liter
1 pound = .45 kilogram

Conversion from Fahrenheit to
Celsius: subtract 32 and then
multiply the remainder by 5/9

Printed in the United States of America. ISBN 0-8167-2913-1
10 9 8 7 6 5 4 3 2 1

Contents

Introduction

Easter is here! It's a celebration of new life. Spring's bright daffodils are in bloom. Baby chicks and bunnies are being born. And for many boys and girls, there are baskets of treats and colorful eggs to be found on Easter morning. The symbols and customs of Easter center around growth, warmth, birth, and joy.

Long ago, people worshiped a goddess of spring called *Eostre*. Easter's name probably came from this ancient symbol of new life. The day on which Easter falls changes each year. It occurs on the first Sunday after the first full moon after the first day of spring. All around the globe, people observe spring's arrival. Our Easter holiday is just one of the world's celebrations of the season of rebirth in nature.

Eggs, bunnies, and flowers are the most popular signs of Easter. We love Easter eggs for their beautiful colors and the fun they provide. But their real meaning is a celebration of the new life held inside an egg. Our Easter Bunny is famous for delivering eggs and gifts on Easter morning. Easter flowers — lilies, tulips, daffodils — are beautiful symbols of nature's rebirth.

This book is filled with crafts, recipes, games, and facts about Easter. They will add fun and special times to your holiday.

Easter Eggs

What kind of Easter-egg artist are you? A beginner — or an eggs-pert? The following tips will add to your fun and skill in decorating eggs.

Boiling Eggs

To make hard-boiled eggs without any cracks, follow these steps:

1. Bring eggs to room temperature.

2. Carefully place eggs in a large pot, then cover with water.

3. Bring water to a full boil. Using potholders, remove pot from heat, cover it with a lid, and let stand for about 25 minutes. (Ask an adult for help, if you're not allowed to use the stove by yourself.)

4. Rinse eggs in cold water.

Decorating Hard-Boiled Eggs

Wax Crayons   Before dying your eggs, draw letters or designs on them with crayons. The wax in the crayon will resist the dye, resulting in a colored egg with a pretty design.

Onion Skins   Onion skins are an old-fashioned way of dying Easter eggs. Boiling the skins produces a soft brown dye. Wrapping an egg in onion skins results in an interesting marble effect. Cover a raw egg with onion skins, wrap the egg in a cloth, then tie the cloth tightly with string. Hard boil the egg in its wrapping. Unwrap your egg when completely cool.

Striped Eggs   Before dying the eggs, cut thin strips of masking tape, each about three inches long. Tape the strips around the eggs. Dye the eggs, then let them dry completely before removing tape. The result is a colored egg with white stripes.

Polka-Dot Eggs   Use a white egg or a dry colored egg. Pour a small amount of non-toxic tempera paint into a small container. Dip the end of a new pencil eraser in the paint. Print the egg with polka dots from the end of the eraser.

Illustrated Eggs   Use non-toxic felt-tip markers to draw brightly colored designs on your eggs. Make up your own designs or draw an Easter symbol, like a rabbit, a flower, or a sun.

7

continued...

Blowing Eggs

You can make pretty Easter eggs that last for years by using hollow eggs. Here's how to prepare your hollow eggs:

1. Hold the egg firmly in your hand, or set it in an egg cup.

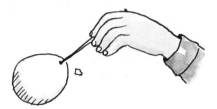

2. Gently pierce one end of the egg with the sharp point of a darning needle. Turn the egg over and pierce the other end. Make the second hole slightly larger.

3. Push the needle inside the larger hole to break the yolk. Stir up the insides.

4. Hold the egg over a bowl. Blow into the smaller hole until the inside of the egg comes out of the shell and into the bowl. The insides can be saved and used for cooking.

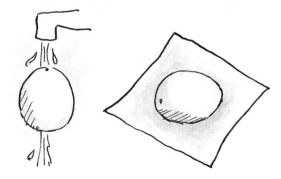

5. Hold the egg under a faucet and run a gentle stream of water through the shell. Shake the water out to clean the inside of the shell.

6. Let the egg dry thoroughly.

Using Hollow Eggs

Filled Eggs   After coloring a hollow egg, put tiny candies through the larger hole. If necessary, make the hole a bit bigger. Tape the hole closed and give the filled egg to someone special as an Easter present.

Hanging Eggs   After dying or decorating the eggs, hang them from a mobile or from the ceiling. Break a toothpick in half and tie a string around the middle of it. Push the stick into the larger hole in the shell. Pull on the string so that the toothpick lodges inside the shell. You now have a hanger for your egg.

Egg Tree   Prepare up to 10 blown eggs with string hangers. Find a fallen tree branch or get permission to prune off a small branch from a tree. Put the branch in a bowl or tin can. Add pebbles or dirt around the base of the branch to make it stand up. Hang the eggs from the branches of the tree.

Popcorn Sculpture

This fluffy, puffy bunny is made out of popcorn. It is fun to make and great to eat. Add a circle of colored eggs, and you'll have a perfect centerpiece for your Easter table.

You Will Need

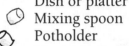

2 quarts popped corn
1/4 cup melted butter or margarine
1 package regular marshmallows
   (10-ounce bag)
Pink jellybeans and gumdrops
1/4 cup light corn syrup

Large mixing bowl
Large saucepan
Dish or platter
Mixing spoon
Potholder
Measuring cup

Steps

1. Measure 2 quarts of popped corn into a large mixing bowl.

2. Melt butter or margarine in a large saucepan over low heat. Stir in the marshmallows and melt thoroughly. Add the light corn syrup to mixture. Remove from heat. (*Caution:* Always use a potholder when working at the stove, and ask for adult help, if you're not allowed to use the stove by yourself.)

3. Pour the mixture over the popcorn. Stir until the popcorn is evenly coated.

4. While the popcorn is still warm, but not hot, mold it into the shape of a bunny. Make one large oval ball for the body. Add a smaller ball for the head. Put a very small ball on the back for a tail. Shape two long ears and attach them to the top of the head.

5. Push two pink jellybeans into the face for eyes. Add a pink gumdrop for a nose.

6. Set your bunny sculpture on a dish or platter and surround it with colored eggs and jellybeans. Later on Easter Day, you can eat your pretty centerpiece as a snack.

Easter Games

Here are four games to play with your family or friends on Easter Day.

Egg Roll

There are many ways to roll an egg, but this is the silliest and the most fun! Ask the players to line up their eggs at a starting line on the grass. (Or if the weather is bad, roll the eggs on a carpet indoors.) The goal is to be the first to get your egg across the finish line. The tricky part is that you have to roll the egg by pushing it along with your nose!

Count the Jellybeans

Fill a glass jar with jellybeans. Before everyone starts eating them, have a guessing contest. Ask the members of your family to guess how many jellybeans are in the jar. Write down their answers. Then count the jellybeans. Award a prize to the one who comes closest.

Spoon Relay

Set up two relay teams. Give each runner a spoon. Mark off a starting line and a midpoint in your yard. One player from each team must run with an Easter egg balanced on the spoon from the starting line to the midpoint and back. Then the player transfers the egg from his or her spoon to the next runner's spoon without using hands. The winning team is the one that does the relay in the fastest time without dropping the egg — and that's not easy! You may have to go through several relays and several cracked eggs before a team manages to win.

Scavenger Hunt

The players can work in teams or alone in this scavenger hunt. The goal is to find natural (not synthetic) objects that begin with each letter of the phrase H-A-P-P-Y E-A-S-T-E-R. The first person or team to bring in eleven natural objects starting with the correct letters wins.

Bubble-Mania

Spring arrives with warm, windy weather. It's a perfect time for blowing bubbles. This year, make bigger, better bubbles than ever with these homemade blowers and bubble solution. The fantastic results will give you and your friends a case of bubble-mania.

Materials

6 tablespoons liquid dishwashing detergent
6 tablespoons glycerin (from a drugstore)
2 cups lukewarm water
Flat, shallow container (baking pan, wash basin)
Large spoon or whisk
Measuring cup and spoons

Several feet of bendable wire
  (plastic-coated works well)
Plastic straws
Tape

Steps

1. Combine water, detergent, and glycerin in a flat, shallow container. Mix well with spoon or whisk.

2. Bend wire into the shape of a bubble blower. For large bubbles, make a loop up to six inches in diameter.

3. For another kind of blower, bundle together four to six straws. Fasten them together with two strips of tape. Make sure the ends of the straws are even.

4. To use the wire blower, dip its flat surface into the bubble solution. Carefully lift it up with a film of solution across the loop. Move the blower through the air until a bubble forms.

5. To use the straw blower, dip one end of the straws into the bubble solution. Lift the straws out and blow through the clean end.

What is the biggest bubble you can make? What is the most beautiful? Bet you catch bubble-mania!

A Peter Rabbit Puppet

Beatrix Potter grew up in a big, gloomy house in the city of London. Although she had no playmates, Beatrix had lots to do. She drew and painted and wrote down stories. In the summer when her family went north to Scotland, Beatrix spent her days drawing country homes, the animals, and the plants that surrounded her.

One beautifully illustrated story, about a rabbit named Peter, was written for a child too ill to get out of bed. Today that same story, *The Tale of Peter Rabbit*, is the best-loved bunny tale of all time!

You can make your own Peter Rabbit puppet. Then, try Flopsy, Mopsy, and Cottontail, too!

Materials
Construction paper
    Pink 6"x 12"
    Brown 6"x 12"
    Blue 3"x 3"
    Green scraps for shoes
Glue
Scissors

Steps

1. Trace and cut out all pattern pieces on the facing page. Fold the brown construction paper in half to trace Peter's body.

2. Lay the pink paper for the cylinder flat. Glue other pattern pieces to the center as shown in Figure A. (Do not glue down the arms.) Use brown for the body, blue for the jacket, pink scraps for the inner ears and nose, and green scraps for the shoes.

Figure A

3. Use markers or crayons to add details to the face.

4. Wait for the pieces to dry. Then shape the pink paper into a cylinder. Staple at the back, top, and bottom, as shown in Figure B.

Figure B

GLUE

Place along folded edge of paper

Thumbprint Cookies

The secret to these yummy cookies is your thumbprint. Push your thumb into a ball of dough. Fill each print with a different flavor of jam. The result is a batch of cookies as colorful as a garden of spring flowers.

You Will Need

1/2 cup butter, softened
3/4 cup granulated sugar
2 eggs
1/2 teaspoon vanilla extract
$1\frac{3}{4}$ cups flour
1 teaspoon baking powder
1/4 teaspoon baking soda
1/4 teaspoon salt
Vegetable shortening
Red jam (cherry, strawberry, raspberry)
Blue jam (grape, blueberry, blackberry)
Yellow jam (orange marmalade, apricot)

Large mixing bowl
Small mixing bowl
Mixing spoon
Small spoon
Measuring cup
Measuring spoons
Flour sifter
Cookie sheet
Spatula
Potholder
Wire rack
Plate

Steps

1. Combine soft butter, sugar, and vanilla extract in a large mixing bowl. Make a light, creamy mixture by mixing with the back of a mixing spoon. Beat two eggs into the mixture.

2. In a small mixing bowl, sift together the flour, baking powder, baking soda, and salt. Add dry ingredients to large bowl. Mix well.

3. Chill dough in refrigerator for 30 minutes.

4. Set the oven at 350° F. Ask an adult to help you. Lightly grease the cookie sheet with vegetable shortening.

5. Remove dough from refrigerator. Roll pieces of dough between your palms into one-inch balls. Dust your hands with flour, if necessary. Set balls of dough on cookie sheet about two inches apart.

6. Press your thumb into each ball, leaving a hole in the center. Fill each thumbprint with a different color of jam.

7. Ask an adult to help you with this step. Bake cookies for 15 minutes or until golden brown. Use a potholder to remove from oven and let the cookies cool on a wire rack.

8. Use a spatula to place the cookies on a pretty plate. Serve these cookies to your guests on Easter Day.

Eggheads

These eggheads grow a crop of green hair. You can give them a short crew cut or let their hair grow long, long, long! Whatever their hair style, eggheads make great Easter gifts. Remember to prepare them at least a week or two ahead of time.

Materials

Half a hollow eggshell or half a plastic egg
Sturdy paper
Tape
Colored pens or markers

Potting soil
Grass seed
Ruler
Water

Steps

1. Prepare a hollow egg (see page 8). Then carefully cut off the top half of the shell. Or separate a hollow plastic egg into halves.

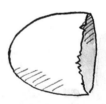

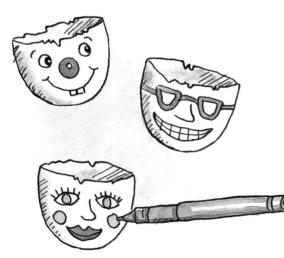

2. Draw features for the face. Give your egghead eyes, eyebrows, a nose, and a mouth. Add rosy cheeks, dimples, and a chin, if you want. Markers work well on an eggshell; pens work better on plastic eggs.

3. Make a stand for the egghead from sturdy paper. Cut a strip of paper one inch wide and four inches long. Overlap the ends half an inch and tape them together. Decorate the stand by drawing on a tie or a necklace.

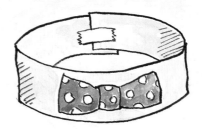

4. Fill the egg almost to the top with potting soil. Sprinkle grass seed over the soil.

5. Set the egghead in the sun. Sprinkle lightly with water every day. In about a week, the grass will begin to grow. Soon you'll need to give your egghead a haircut.

Get the Yolk?

If a red rooster laid a white egg, what kind of chick would hatch out?

None. Roosters don't lay eggs.

What was the hen with bad eyesight doing in the garden?

Sitting on an eggplant

What do you call it when two hens switch nests?

An eggs-change

If you cross a baby chick with an alley cat, what do you get?

A peeping Tom

Why did the turkey cross the road?

To prove he wasn't chicken

What did Snow White call her chicken?

Egg White

Why did Humpty Dumpty have a great fall?

To make up for a bad summer

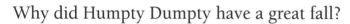

What did Humpty Dumpty die of?

Shell shock

If joke is spelled "j-o-k-e,"
and if poke is spelled "p-o-k-e,"
how do you spell
the white part of an egg?

A-l-b-u-m-e-n (the yolk is the yellow part)

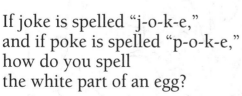

Spring Potpourri

Recycle your Easter flowers by using the petals to make a potpourri. A potpourri (PO-poor-ree) is a mixture of dried flower petals, leaves, and spices. After being aged in a jar, the potpourri adds a sweet smell to a closet or room.

Materials:

Flower petals
Flower and herb leaves
Orrisroot powder (from a drugstore)
Spice mixture (cloves, allspice, nutmeg)
White paper

Measuring cup and spoons
Spoon
Bowl
Glass jar with screw-on lid

Steps

1. Gather petals from spring flowers that have finished blooming. Choose a variety of colors, if possible. Pick small leaves from the flowers as well as leaves from herbs, like lavender and thyme.

2. Spread out the petals and leaves on a sheet of white paper. Leave them to dry in a well-aired place out of the sun. Turn the leaves occasionally until they are dry to the touch.

3. Using a measuring cup, measure the amount of mixture you have. Then put it in a bowl. Add one teaspoon of orrisroot for every pint (2 cups) of dried petals and leaves. Then add one teaspoon of mixed spices (such as cloves, allspice, nutmeg) for every pint of the mixture. Gently stir all the ingredients with a spoon.

4. Store the mixture in a glass jar with a screw-on lid. Let it set for six weeks.

5. Open the lid and smell the potpourri. Pour a small portion into a container to add a nice spring fragrance to any room.

The egg is a natural wonder. Its shell is lightweight, but strong. Its shape is unusual, but practical. The following experiments use eggs to show principles of science. The results are interesting, fun, and egg-cellent!

The Unbreakable Egg

You Will Need

An egg

Steps

1. Choose an egg without cracks in its shell. Take off any rings you might be wearing. Hold the egg over your kitchen sink, just in case of a spill.

2. Put the egg in the palm of your hand and close your fingers tightly around it. Now squeeze, as hard as you can! The egg won't break, no matter how hard you try.

Why It Happens

You normally crack an egg by hitting one small area of its shell against a hard surface. When you squeeze an egg in your hand, the force spreads over the entire surface of the shell. Nature designed the egg like a three-dimensional arch. It is one of the strongest forms in nature and architecture.

The Spinning Egg

Steps

1. Ask a friend to mix up the four eggs so that you can't tell which is the hard-boiled one. Announce that you can pick out the hard-boiled egg.

2. Put an egg on a plate. Spin it around like a top on the plate surface. Do the same for the other three eggs.

3. Three of the eggs will not spin easily. One will twirl around with ease. This one is the hard-boiled egg.

Why It Happens

The hard-boiled egg behaves like a solid. It has a fixed balance point and spins like a top. The raw eggs are filled with fluid and behave like a liquid. It is difficult to make them begin to spin. These eggs also take longer to come to a stop.

continued...

The Rubber Egg

Steps

1. Set the egg in the bottom of the glass. Add enough vinegar to completely cover the egg.

2. Wait for 36 to 48 hours.

3. Carefully remove the egg from the vinegar. Gently squeeze it. You have created a rubber egg!

Why It Happens

An eggshell is made of calcium, which makes the shell hard. The acid in the vinegar dissolved the calcium in the shell, leaving a soft, rubbery substance.

Trivia Quiz

1. What event takes place on the White House lawn every year at Easter?

2. Where did the idea of an Easter bunny come from?

3. What name is the Easter Bunny given in the well-known song that begins "Here comes . . ."?

continued...

4. What famous rabbit did Beatrix Potter write about? (Can you remember?)

5. In what book did a stuffed rabbit become real?

6. How long does it take a hen to produce an egg? How long does it take for a fertilized egg to hatch into a chick? How many eggs can a chicken lay in a year?

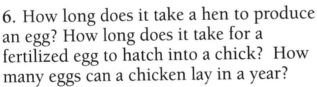

7. On what day is Easter celebrated? (Can you remember?)

Answers to Trivia Quiz

1. Every Easter, there is an egg-rolling contest on the White House lawn. The President of the United States gives prizes to the winners.

2. Easter is named after the goddess Eostre, and she had a hare (a cousin of the rabbit) as a pet.

3. The name is Peter Cottontail.

4. Peter Rabbit is the famous bunny. Beatrix Potter, an English author, wrote and illustrated a book called *The Tale of Peter Rabbit*. Peter is famous for his adventures in Mr. McGregor's garden.

5. *The Velveteen Rabbit* by Margery Williams tells the story of a stuffed rabbit that becomes real through his owner's love.

6. A hen produces a finished egg in 24 to 25 hours. The incubation period for a chicken egg is 21 days. Hens can lay up to 250 eggs in a year.

7. Easter is celebrated on the first Sunday after the first full moon after the first day of spring.

An Easter Basket

The Easter bunny has lots of sweet surprises for you to find on Easter morning. Why not put them in a beautiful handmade basket? Use any color you like, or a combination of colors.

Materials

Construction paper (12" x 18")   Scissors
Pencil   Glue
Ruler   Paper clips

Steps

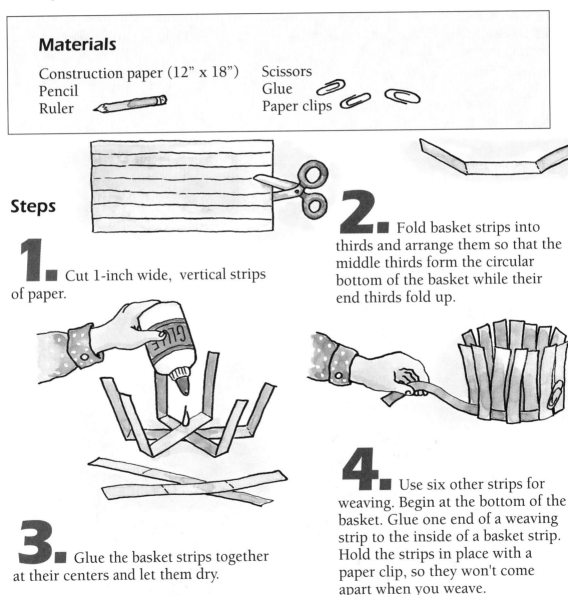

1. Cut 1-inch wide, vertical strips of paper.

2. Fold basket strips into thirds and arrange them so that the middle thirds form the circular bottom of the basket while their end thirds fold up.

3. Glue the basket strips together at their centers and let them dry.

4. Use six other strips for weaving. Begin at the bottom of the basket. Glue one end of a weaving strip to the inside of a basket strip. Hold the strips in place with a paper clip, so they won't come apart when you weave.

5. Bring the weaving strip outside of the next basket strip, then take it inside the next basket strip, and so on until it meets its other end. Glue the ends of the weaving strip together inside the basket. Let dry.

6. Remove the paper clip. Start your next weaving strip, following Step 5. Use this same method for weaving the rest of the strips.

7. Apply glue to the back of a new strip and wrap this strip around the top of your basket. Hold this strip in place with a paper clip while it dries.

8. Cut the last strip to measure 15 inches. Glue each end to the inside of the basket at opposite sides. Let your beautiful, new Easter basket dry before using.

The Magic Egg

This magic trick will make you look eggs-tremely clever. On your command, an egg will mysteriously float in a glass of water. Only you will know the scientific secret to the trick.

You Will Need

2 raw eggs   Water
2 large drinking glasses   Mixing spoon
4 –5 tablespoons salt

Steps

1. Fill each glass three-quarters full with water. Set one glass to the side.

2. Add 4 tablespoons of salt to the second glass. Mix thoroughly. Gently drop an egg into the second glass. If it does not float, remove it and add more salt. Experiment until you have enough salt in the water to make the egg float. Remove the egg. Allow it to dry.

3. When your audience is assembled, explain that one of the two eggs you have is magical and obeys your commands. Pass the eggs around for everyone to see that the eggs are identical.

4. Gently drop one egg into the glass of plain water. Predict that it will sink to the bottom.

5. Drop the second egg into the salt water. As you do, command it to float. Like magic, the egg will obey you!

Why It Happens

A heavier liquid will support more weight than a lighter liquid. The salty water weighs more than the plain water. It holds the egg up so it floats. The same principle works for swimmers in fresh water and sea water. The salty sea water makes a swimmer float more easily than he or she would in fresh water.

Easter Word Hunt

This puzzle is a hiding place for Easter words. It is fun and easy for you to make. But if you're tricky, it can be a challenge for others to solve! Give a prize to the person who can find all the words you've hidden in this Easter word hunt.

Materials

Sheet of white poster board	Scissors
Scrap paper	Old magazines and newspapers
Pencil	Glue
Ruler	Markers

Steps

 Make a list of all the Easter words you can think of — for example: bunny, eggs, chocolate, basket, and so on. Try to think up at least 15 to 20 words.

2. On another piece of scrap paper, draw a grid that has 15 blocks across and 15 blocks down. Use a ruler and pencil to measure and draw the lines.

3. Fill in the grid with your list of Easter words. Hide the words by writing them in different ways. Try writing them (a) from left to right; (b) from right to left; (c) from top to bottom; (d) from bottom to top; (e) at a diagonal from top to bottom; (f) at a diagonal from bottom to top.

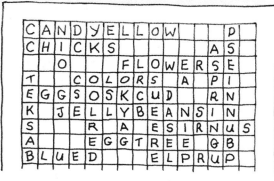

4. After all your Easter words are hidden, fill in the remaining boxes with any letters you choose. You can fill in a few boxes with pictures of eggs or rabbits.

5. Now copy your grid onto poster board. You can fill in the letters of the puzzle with markers. Another way is to cut letters from old magazines or newspapers. Make piles of the alphabet letters to use in the puzzle. Then glue the letters onto the boxes of your puzzle. The effect is even more confusing and mysterious.

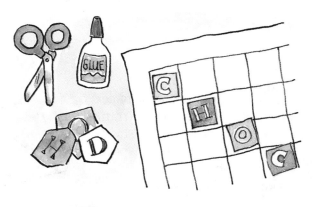

6. On Easter, ask the members of your family to write down how many Easter words they can find in your puzzle. Explain the different ways the words have been written. Award the winner a special egg or piece of candy.

 # Easter Lollipops

Set up your own candy kitchen for Easter. You'll agree that these lollipops are the best you've ever tasted — because you made them yourself! Remember, an adult's help is needed with the stove.

You Will Need

2 cups sugar
1/2 cup light corn syrup
1/2 cup water
1/2 teaspoon flavoring extract
   (vanilla, cinnamon, or peppermint)
Different colors of food coloring
Lollipop sticks
Heavy saucepan
Mixing spoon

Serving spoon or small ladle
Measuring cup
Measuring spoons
Candy thermometer
Cookie sheets or sheets of
   aluminum foil
Butter or margarine
Bowls
Plastic wrap
Potholder

Steps

1. Butter the cookie sheets or sheets of aluminum foil. Arrange the lollipop sticks on the sheets, leaving about 2 inches of space between them. The recipe will make about 36 lollipops.

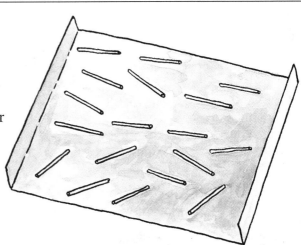

2. Combine the sugar, light corn syrup, and water in a heavy saucepan. Stir to mix well.

3. With an adult's help, attach a candy thermometer to the pan. Cook the mixture until the thermometer reads 300° F. You do not have to stir the mixture.

4. Using a potholder, remove pan from heat. Add the flavoring extract to the mixture.

5. If you want all the lollipops to be the same color, add several drops of one food coloring to the mixture. If you want different colors for the lollipops, separate the mixture into bowls and add colorings.

6. Use a serving spoon or a small ladle to pour the mixture onto the tops of the sticks.

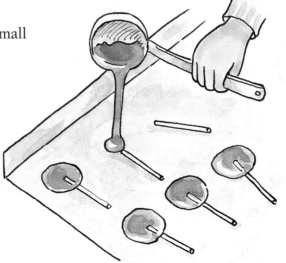

7. Let cool for 10 to 15 minutes. Remove the lollipops from the sheets. Wrap each in plastic wrap.

8. Give lollipops from your very own candy kitchen as Easter presents.

Easter Flowers

Many spring flowers — like tulips, daffodils, and crocuses — grow from bulbs. The bulbs are hard, brown, and covered with a papery shell. You don't need an outdoor garden to have Easter flowers. Some bulbs can be grown indoors in pots full of pebbles and water.

A beautiful spring flower called the narcissus is especially easy to grow indoors. If you plant these bulbs two or three weeks before Easter, you'll have fresh-blooming flowers for your holiday.

Materials

4 or 5 narcissus bulbs (ask for a "tender" variety, such as "Paper White," at the garden store)
Pot or bowl (about 6 inches deep)

Pebbles, gravel, or marble chips to fill the bowl
Pitcher of water

2. Set the bulbs on top of the pebbles with the root, or flat side, down.

Steps

1. Fill a pot or bowl two-thirds full with pebbles or stone chips.

3. Pour in enough water to reach the top of the pebbles or chips.

4. Add more pebbles or chips around the bulbs. Leave the tops of the bulbs showing.

5. Set the pot near a sunny window.

6. Check the water level in the bowl occasionally. Add water to keep the level up to the bottom of the bulbs.

7. Your narcissus bulbs will bloom into beautiful flowers in two to four weeks.

Making Rainbows

Spring brings us one of nature's best surprises — the rainbow. Most of the time, sunlight seems white to us. But it is actually made up of all the colors of the rainbow. A rainbow appears when the sun shines on raindrops in the air. The raindrops bend and reflect the sunlight into many colors — violet, indigo, blue, green, yellow, orange, and red.

You don't have to wait for one of nature's rare light shows. You can make a rainbow yourself, indoors, on a sunny day.

Materials

Shallow pan (cake pan or ice-cube tray works well)
Small mirror
Water

Steps

1. Find a good location for the experiment. Three things are necessary: a window with the sun shining through it; a table or windowsill near the window, on which to set a pan of water; and a light-colored wall at a right angle to the window.

2. Place a shallow pan near the window so that direct sunlight falls on it. Fill the pan with water.

3. Set a small mirror near one end of the pan. Move the mirror and the pan until they are in a position to catch the sun's rays and reflect them onto the wall.

4. The mirror and the water act on sunlight in the same way that a rainbow is formed. The "white" sunlight is broken down into its colors. If you move the pan close to the wall, you'll get a small rainbow with intense colors. If you move the pan farther away, you'll get a bigger rainbow with less intense colors.

5. If the sun is shining, make a rainbow for your family on Easter Day.

Hot Cross Buns

Hot cross buns are named after the cross of white icing that decorates them. These buns are an old tradition of the Easter season. In England, they used to be baked early in the morning on Good Friday, the Friday before Easter Sunday. People bought them, fresh and hot, from street vendors.

Try this easy recipe for hot cross buns. They may become an Easter tradition in your home, too. (Note that adult help is necessary when using the stove and oven.)

You Will Need

2 1-pound loaves of frozen bread dough
1/2 cup raisins, softened in warm water
1 teaspoon cinnamon
1/2 cup confectioners' sugar
2 teaspoons milk
Vegetable shortening
Large mixing bowl
Small mixing bowl

Mixing spoon
Measuring cup
Measuring spoons
Baking sheet
Wax paper
Scissors or a knife
Small saucepan
Potholders
Spoon

Steps

1. Thaw the frozen dough according to directions. When thawed, combine dough with raisins and cinnamon in a large bowl.

2. Divide the dough into about 20 pieces. Shape the pieces into round buns.

3. Grease a baking sheet with vegetable shortening. Place the buns on the sheet, about 2 inches apart. Cover the sheet with wax paper and set it in a warm place. Let the dough rise until it doubles in size.

4. Preheat oven to 350° F.

5. Just before baking, remove the wax paper. Snip a cross in the top of each bun with scissors or a knife, cutting the dough an inch deep.

6. Bake buns for 15 to 20 minutes or until light brown. Use potholders to remove the baking sheet from the oven.

7. Warm the milk in a small saucepan. Be careful not to let it boil. Pour the confectioners' sugar into a small mixing bowl. Add the warm milk. Stir until smooth.

8. Using the thin end of a spoon, put a cross of icing on top of each bun. Follow the cross outline baked into the dough.

9. Serve your hot cross buns fresh for an Easter treat.

Homemade Butter Eggs

Have you ever made butter? If not, this Easter is a perfect time to learn. You can make "butter eggs" to serve with hot cross buns on Easter morning.

Children were often responsible for making butter in early America. They used cream that was skimmed off milk. The cream was poured into tall, wooden buckets called churns. It was hard work to churn the milk into butter.

This recipe for making butter is lots of fun, especially if you share the "shaking" part of it with a brother, sister, or friend.

You Will Need

2 cups heavy cream
1/4 teaspoon salt
1 quart-size glass jar with a screw-on lid
Large mixing bowl

4–5 ice cubes
Small dish
Spoon
Measuring cup and spoons

Steps

1. Set the cream and the glass jar in a warm place for two hours. Use a sunny windowsill or a place near the stove.

2. Pour the warm cream into the glass jar. Close the lid tightly. Put one hand on the bottom of the jar and the other hand on the top of the jar. Holding it securely, shake the jar up and down for 10 to 20 minutes. Take turns with someone.

3. You can stop shaking the jar when the butter begins to stick together and form a solid. Open the lid, and pour off the liquid buttermilk. Scrape the butter out of the jar into a mixing bowl.

4. Make sure your hands are clean for this step. Add four or five ice cubes to the bowl and wait for them to melt a little. With your fingers, work the icy water into the butter to chill it. Then pour out the ice cubes and water.

5. Add the salt to the butter, mixing it in evenly.

6. Divide the butter into six parts. Shape each lump into an egg with your hands. Place the butter eggs on a dish. Put the butter in the refrigerator to harden.

7. Serve your homemade butter with hot cross buns (see the recipe on page 44) or at Easter dinner.

Happy Easter!